A Salty Tale

Written by Susan Markowitz Meredith

Illustrated by Kelvin Hucker

Like any cook worth his salt, I know how to make flapjacks. I mean the kind that'd satisfy a hungry lumberjack, including Paul Bunyan himself.

Of course, no one can eat like Paul. That's 'cause no one's quite as big. Who else has legs the size of tree trunks and hands as large as five-gallon jugs?

I remember the year our logging crew thinned out the North Woods pretty good. Paul decided it was time to leave our Big Onion River camp and head for the great West.

"Plenty of trees there," Paul told us.

The day we left, Paul and his blue ox, Babe, went on ahead. When we reached Utah in the late afternoon, Paul had already set up camp next to a great big lake.

We couldn't help but notice the giant basket of potatoes sittin' there.

"Babe and I picked up a few spuds along the way," said Paul.

Babe must've hauled that basket across four states. I tell ya, that big ox would do anything for Paul. It's no wonder. Paul had raised him since he was a calf—long before he turned blue during that Winter of the Blue Snow. But that's another story.

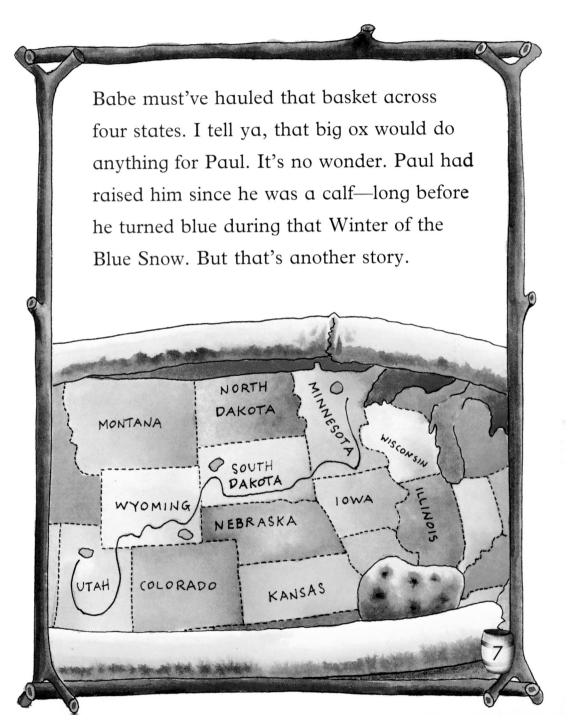

Anyway, we kinda guessed that Paul wanted potatoes for dinner. Then when he started eyein' those log-size sausages on our wagons, we figured out the rest.

I was a cookee in those days, which means I was an assistant cook. There were 83 of us. Our head cook was Paul's cousin, Huge Horace. He came over from England to work right after Big Joe, our old cook, left.

Huge Horace gathered us around him. "Let's give the bangers 'n' mash a go," he said.

Since none of the cookees understood English from England, we gave Horace a quizzical look. Then we sorta decided mash must be what you did to potatoes and bangin' was the noise sausages made on a hot griddle.

With that problem settled, we were ready to start dinner.

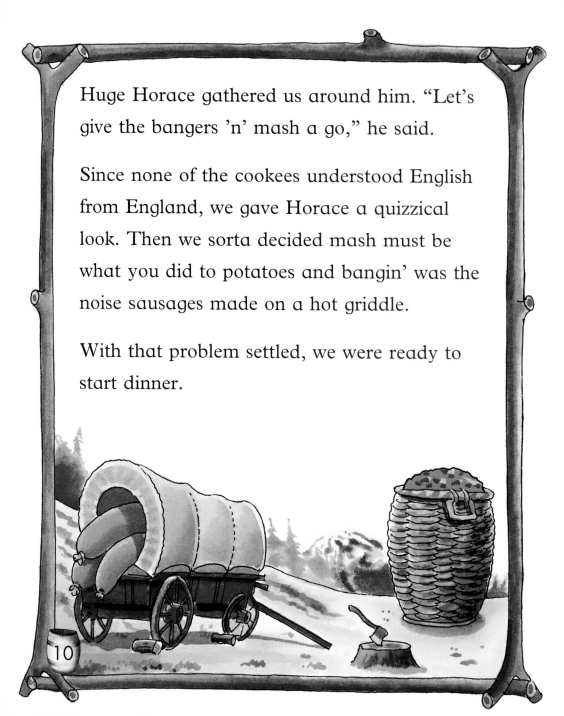

11

Except we had another problem. There wasn't a pot big enough to cook it in.

"Leave that to me," said Ole the Blacksmith. He picked up a handful of soil and looked at it. "Time to do some copper mining," he said. Then off he went to find a good diggin' place.

Mining was nothing new to Ole. He would open a new iron mine every time Babe needed a set of shoes.

Before too long, Ole had found copper and fashioned a nice big pot.

As soon as he brought it back to camp, we carried it over to the lake and filled it with water.

Then we lugged the pot back and set it over the fire. We spent the better part of an hour dumpin' all those potatoes in.

I must say they cooked up real good. Horace
added a hefty chunk of salt from the big
block he always kept by the fire.

Then we mashed the potatoes nice and smooth with our riverboat paddle wheel. That's the one Paul got when he went down the Mississippi to sell logs. But that's another story.

Keeping with English custom, Horace piled the potatoes into a big mound. Then we helped him stand up the sausages all around it.

Folks in Nevada later told us they could see our bangers 'n' mash on the eastern horizon.

What a dinner! I remember Paul and the lumberjacks sittin' around the acre-wide table with that mountain of vittles in the center. And who can forget that horse-drawn wagon totin' the giant gravy pitcher around?

Afterward, while we were clearin' the table, Babe came from out of nowhere and grabbed a sausage.

Paul was a little vexed but mostly amused. We sure laughed as he chased that feisty blue ox around the camp. Then he pulled Babe down, and they began rollin' this way and that.

21

It was bound to happen. Paul and Babe fell on top of that big block of salt by the fire and crushed it. Before you could say "salted peanuts," there was so much salt in the air it looked like a dust storm.

Slowly the salt settled—boy, did it settle! As far as the eye could see, the land was covered in salt and had all dried up.

And that great big lake nearby? Yep, salt settled into that too.

The next morning we packed up camp and headed west. As I looked back, I knew the Utah landscape would never be the same.

That big lake is now called the Great Salt Lake. And all that white sand by it is called the Great Salt Lake Desert. Oh, and remember Ole's copper mine? It's still in use today.